Journey to a
Free Land

The story of Nicodemus, the first all black town west of the Mississippi

Written by **Theda Robinson Robertson**
Illustrated by **Wilbert Fobbs**

Library of Congress Cataloging-in-Publication Data:

Robertson, Theda Robinson, 1931-
Journey to a free land : the story of Nicodemus, the first all Black
town west of the Mississippi / by Theda Robinson Robertson ;
illustrated by Wilbert Fobbs.
p. cm.
ISBN-13: 978-0-9705721-6-5
ISBN-10: 0-9705721-6-6
1. Nicodemus (Kan.)--History--Juvenile literature. 2. African
Americans--Kansas--Nicodemus--History--Juvenile literature.
3. African American pioneers--Kansas--Nicodemus--History
--Juvenile literature. 4. Frontier and pioneer life--Kansas
--Nicodemus--Juvenile literature. 5. African Americans--Kansas
--Nicodemus--Biography--Juvenile literature. 6. Nicodemus (Kan.)
--Biography--Juvenile literature.   I. Title.
F689.N5R63 2006

978.1'163--dc22

2006013768

Sally was excited. She was going to the Emancipation Celebration! Every year in *Nicodemus, Kansas,* the people who lived in and around the city gathered at the local church to celebrate the fact that slavery was over. After the church services, hundreds of blacks and whites from all over gathered in a nearby beautiful *grove* to continue their celebration. There were baseball games, boxing matches, music, and dancing.

What Sally enjoyed most was the carnival and the big ferris wheel. Some of the blacks who lived in Nicodemus set up food stands where they sold *sumptuous* fried chicken, barbeque, lemonade, and homemade ice cream.

Mrs. Goins and her husband Dan lived in a large stone house on the first hill on the main road in town. As Sally played with her friends, she looked up and saw Mrs. Goins sitting on her porch. "Oh," said Sally, "there's Mrs. Goins." Sally was always happy to see Mrs. Goins because she always had such wonderful stories to tell.

Everyone who knew Sally knew she was a very *inquisitive* child. She wanted to learn everything, especially history. She was fascinated with words, and what she wanted most was her very own dictionary. She would tell her friends, "If I had my own dictionary, then I could learn every word in it and have the biggest vocabulary in the State of Kansas." So when Sally saw Mrs. Goins she knew she was about to learn another important history lesson, one she would enjoy, one she would remember, one she would repeat to those who came after her. She understood at a very young age how important it was to learn and pass on important facts about black history. There were no books about black history when Sally was young, but she had Mrs. Goins and that was good enough for Sally.

Mrs. Goins was tall and brown, with a beautiful, full head of long, silvery white hair and kind black eyes that sparkled and danced whenever she saw young children. She loved all the children in Nicodemus because they kept her company. She would tell the children stories about what it was like when black people were slaves in *Kentucky*. After Emancipation a group of former slaves came to Nicodemus, Kansas from Kentucky with a group of people who were looking for the land that was free.

As Sally and the other children rushed up the hill they knew by the glint in Mrs. Goins' eyes that something exciting was about to happen. Then, Mrs. Goins began to speak.

Mrs. Goins began. "Children, a long, long time ago, two men came to the church one Sunday morning in the late summer to tell the members about the promised land that was free in Kansas. The Reverend Benjamin 'Pap' Singleton and Mr. W. R. Hill had been to Nicodemus, Kansas and had seen this promised land. They said it was a wonderful land with lots of large trees along the *Solomon River*."

Sally couldn't help asking. "Why is this place called Nicodemus?" The other children nodded. "Nicodemus was the name of a legendary black slave who later purchased his freedom," Mrs. Goins answered. "This town was named 'Nicodemus' in honor of him and to celebrate and honor the black pioneers who traveled here to find freedom.

"May I continue my story now?" she added, smiling.

"Yes," said all the children politely.

"Reverend Singleton and Mr. Hill told the church people, 'You can build houses from the trees already on the land. And Nicodemus has all kind of wild game such as deer, rabbits, wild turkeys, ducks and pheasants. No one would want for food.' With all the free land in Nicodemus, we would be able to farm our own land and grow all the food we need," explained Mrs. Goins.

"Reverend Singleton and Mr. Hill continued to explained how the people could get to this free land. 'All we need is a little money for the paperwork, so that you can prove that the land is yours,' they said. The people in the church got very excited as they heard this wonderful news.

"Then Mr. Hill said, 'We are planning a trip to Kansas right now. All of you that want to go, start planning. We will be sending out more news about the trip very soon.'"

"Then the people started to hear *rumblings*," said Mrs. Goins. "People were saying that this could be a dangerous trip because some of the white men were very angry about the slaves leaving. They were angry because if their slaves left, the former slave owners would have to pay for the work that the slaves had been doing for free in the fields, as well as all the other jobs the slaves had done for free.

"Some of the slaves' masters tried to scare the slaves. 'A lot of men are watching you leave,' they would tell them. 'Those men are going to follow you, rob you, and beat you up,' they warned. 'You'd be better off staying on the *plantations* here in Kentucky; at least you'll be safe.'

"Shortly after the people heard all these frightening stories, they heard that there were still men like *John Brown*, whose group continued to ride the plains and would protect the people who were leaving in wagon trains for the free land."

"They also heard the government had a group of soldiers called *Buffalo Soldiers* that rode the Kentucky and Kansas *plains* to patrol and watch for trouble. The Buffalo Soldiers were black soldiers especially chosen to protect wagon trains and help develop the West."

"Some of the people discussed their fears with their former masters, who reassured them, saying 'don't be afraid to leave, because President *Abraham Lincoln* has freed all of the slaves to go any place they want.' It made many of the people feel better about the trip."

Mrs. Goins continued. "Soon after that people began to talk about the trip to Kansas. There were posters placed all over town." One poster read:

"'ALL *COLORED* PEOPLE

THAT WANT TO GO TO KANSAS

ON SEPTEMBER 5TH, 1877
CAN DO SO FOR $5.00'''

"Many people on the plantations packed their wagons and started out for this beautiful free land in Kansas. It was a hard trip over the mountains and across the rivers. I don't remember exactly how long the trip took," explained Mrs. Goins.

"The wagons would stop in the evenings and the men would set up camp. Some of the men would go ahead and hunt. They would have lots of meat by the time the wagon train reached the camp."

Mrs. Goins continued to *reminisce.* "The men would make camp fires and the women would cook supper. Then before bedtime, the camp people would sing songs and pray. Some of the people slept on the ground because their wagons were full of supplies, furniture and things they would need when they got to Kansas.

"But they didn't mind. They were willing to endure anything in order to be free."

"The people saw lots of *Native Americans* along the way from a distance," Mrs. Goins continued, "watching the wagons as they traveled along, but they never came near. They later learned that those Native Americans were the friendly *Osage Indians*.

"Many days and nights passed before the wagon train reached Nicodemus. Everyone shouted with glee when they saw the great muddy *Solomon River*."

Mrs. Goins began sitting up and gesturing. She was getting excited. "The leader of the wagon train stopped his wagon and got out," she explained. "He shouted, 'We are here!' Pointing to the ground, he shouted, 'there is Nicodemus!'"

Mrs. Goins looked far above the children's heads, as if she were looking across the Solomon River and seeing the promised land of Nicodemus.

"One of the ladies was confused," continued Mrs. Goins. "This one woman asked, 'Where, what are you talking about? Where is Nicodemus?'"

"'Over yonder, where the smoke is coming from the ground,' the wagon train leader replied. 'The people live underground in *dug outs*. They haven't had time to build their homes.' Dug outs were underground homes that protected the people from the winter weather."

Mrs. Goins continued. "When she saw that the homes were under the ground and didn't look very nice to live in, the lady cried out, 'This is a sad day for me! We left our homes in Kentucky for this?' she said as the tears welled up in her eyes."

"But then she remembered what it had been like to be owned by someone, to not be able to come and go as you please, to have masters make every decision for you, to have your husband and your children sent away forever just because someone else wanted to buy them. She also remembered how some masters whipped their slaves and were very mean to them. Once she thought about what it would be like to go back, that same woman who was upset about living underground exclaimed, 'but at least we are free, free, free!'"

Mrs. Goins smiled and continued. "As the wagons crossed the mighty Solomon River, a man named Mr. Dan Hickman and several other people came out to greet everyone. They were happy to see all the new people. They made camp that night in Nicodemus and told of the hard trip from Kentucky.

"The land was flat and one could see across the plains for miles, it seemed, unlike the trees and mountains back in Kentucky. Several of the people who had made the journey were very upset about Nicodemus and got back in their wagons and turned back to Kentucky, but most stayed on.

"When some of the men started to build homes, a man who already lived in Nicodemus stopped them. He told them it was too late for anyone to start building now. He said, 'You have to prepare for the winter now. Winter is very bad here.' So everyone started building their dug outs.

"The men hunted and cut wood for the winter. The one good thing about dug outs was that these underground homes were warm inside.

"They had been told of the land of plenty, but that was not exactly true," continued Mrs. Goins. "No one told them that the heavy snow would make it very difficult for the men to find meat to last through the winter. Winter came quickly, and everyone began to get frightened that the food might run out.

"Then, the wood started running out. The people were forced to *ration* both the food and the wood. Most of the time they were cold in the dug outs because of the wood rationing, so everyone wore warm clothing all the time.

"There came a night when the people were almost out of food and wood," continued Mrs. Goins. "They didn't know what to do, so they just prayed and went to sleep."

"Imagine the surprise the next evening when the townspeople heard the hooves of what sounded like fifty to one-hundred horses in front of the dug outs. Some peeked out to see what was happening. It was the Osage Indians returning from a hunting trip.

"Someone screamed in fright, 'Oh no, they are here to hurt us!' Everyone was afraid," she told the children.

"But then they saw the Osage Indians dropping sacks of wood and large bundles of grain, dried fish, squash and beans. They weren't here to hurt anyone; they had come to save the black pioneers' lives!

"The men ran out to thank the Osage Indians for their kindness and to see what they had left, but it was too late. The Indians rode off as fast as they had ridden in. They left enough food to last a long, long time."

"Were they able to make it through the winter?" Sally asked Mrs. Goins.

"Oh yes," Mrs. Goins replied. "All of the settlers made it through the winter just fine because of the Indians.

"When spring arrived," she continued, "many more wagons and people arrived in Nicodemus and began to build houses from sod. The houses were called *soddies*." The people of Nicodemus had already built their soddies, so many of them pitched in to help them as they had been helped.

"But something very important was missing. Can you guess what that might be?" Mrs. Goins asked the children.

"A gas station?" asked Sally.

"No," said Mrs. Goins. "There were no cars back then."

"I know!" said Skitzy, Sally's older brother. "A movie theater, so you could go to the show."

Mrs. Goins smiled. "No, there were no theaters then, either."

"What was needed was a church," Mrs. Goins continued. "Nicodemus needed a place for the community to gather and worship. The men built a beautiful church made of sod, just like the houses.

"The Reverend Silas Lee held the first church service. It was a glorious day, as people from near and far came to celebrate their new lives as free people."

"The people kept coming," continued Mrs. Goins. "There was Mr. William Kirtley, who brought twelve books including a Webster dictionary, a speller, an arithmetic book, and many other things needed in order to start a school for the children. Mrs. Jennie Fletcher, a teacher, taught the children in a soddie school that the townspeople had built. The children sat on cut logs made especially for them. They learned reading and arithmetic. Many of the children learned quickly because some of them had parents that had learned reading and math in Kentucky.

"But Mrs. Fletcher taught much more than just reading and arithmetic," explained Mrs. Goins. "She taught about how important it was to be clean, and always instructed every child to be good. 'The town has very good people in it and you must always be good'; Mrs. Fletcher told the children that at least once every day," remembered Mrs. Goins.

A tear formed in Mrs. Goins's eye as she remembered something else. "It wasn't just the Osage Indians that helped us," she explained. "The wonderful thing was that every new group of settlers that came to Nicodemus brought something to those who were already there. Everyone was very poor," she remembered, "and I will never forget that there was a group of 50 people led by Reverend Goodwin who came to Nicodemus. They brought money, horses, and wagons, and they gave generously."

"The town grew and grew as more people came to find the promised land in Kansas," continued Mrs. Goins. "The people who built soddies covered their sod houses with wood, so their homes would be strong enough to protect them during the harsh winters and the hot summers. The town of Nicodemus grew to six hundred people.

"The settlers were happy now. They had built a town that had churches, grocery stores, drug stores, a hotel, a post office and a bank. There were even two newspapers and a doctor. Everyone got alone fine, and the children were very good, as Mrs. Fletcher had instructed them to be.

"But there was one more thing that was missing. Children, can you guess what it might be this time?"

"A playground!" shouted the children in unison.

"No," said Mrs. Goins, her bright eyes laughing. "Nicodemus had everything except a railroad. The townspeople had to travel to Ellis, Kansas, about thirty-five miles away, to get the supplies they needed. A railroad was needed to bring supplies to the town."

She continued, "The men worked to try to get the railroad to come through Nicodemus but all their efforts failed. Not long after that, some of the businesses began to close and Nicodemus had only a few of its first settlers left."

"That is why so many people come every year to Nicodemus," Mrs. Goins explained. We must never forget where we came from and what we have been given to get us to where we are today. As we continue to celebrate our history, we gain courage for the future."

The children looked at Mrs. Goins as she took a fresh hankie from her pocket and wiped tears from her eyes. She looked very sad. "That's all for today children," she said.

The children thanked Mrs. Goins for the story. "When can we hear another one?" asked Sally.

"Come over to my house tomorrow afternoon and we'll sit under the shade tree in my front yard," said Mrs. Goins, brightening up as she saw how interested the children were in the history of Nicodemus.

The children looked forward to seeing Mrs. Goins the next day.

There would be many, many more times when Mrs. Goins would sit out on her front porch in her wheelchair to catch the morning sun while she brushed her long silver hair and told the children of Nicodemus the many stories she remembered about the long journey from Kentucky to Kansas.

Sally would always watch for Mrs. Goins to come out because there was still so much she wanted to learn about Nicodemus, Kansas, and the black pioneers who traveled to their promised land.

GLOSSARY

DO YOU KNOW THESE WORDS?

Colored – the term that was used to describe African Americans.

Dug out – homes that were made by digging a large hole in the ground.

Grove – a small planting of trees.

Inquisitive – to be a person who asks a lot of questions; one who is curious.

Plains – a large area of flat, or level, land.

Plantation – refers to large farms in the South that were worked by enslaved people, as well as by freed blacks right after slavery was ended.

Ration – to give out a certain amount of food or other needed items on a regular basis in order to make sure the items do not run out too quickly.

Reminisce – to fondly remember something pleasant from the past.

Rumblings – a group of complaining voices.

Soddies – houses built from sod, or dirt.

Sumptious – delicious; often refers to food.

DO YOU KNOW THESE PEOPLE?

John Brown – a white man who participated in the Underground Railroad and led military-style attacks designed to force the end of slavery.

Buffalo Soldiers – African American U.S. army groups given the authority by Congress to patrol the West after the Civil War.

Abraham Lincoln – 16th President of the United States who saw the country through the Civil War and ended the institution of slavery.

Native American – people who originally lived in North America.

Osage Indians – Native Americans who lived in Missouri, Arkansas, Kansas, and Oklahoma.

DO YOU KNOW THESE PLACES?

Kansas – 34th U.S. state, admitted to the Union in 1861; located in the center of the United States, it is bordered by Missouri to the east, Oklahoma to the south, Colorado to the west, and Nebraska to the north.

Kentucky – 15th U.S. state, admitted to the Union in 1792; located west of the Appalachian Mountains.

Nicodemus – the first town built by African Americans; located in the state of Kansas.

Solomon River – a river found in northwest and north central Kansas.

For more information on the historic town of Nicodemus…

Visit these websites:

www.legendsofamerica.com/OZ-Nicodemus.html

www.soulofamerica.com/resorts/nicodemus.html

And read these books:

First Dawn, by Judith Miller

Exodusters: Black Migration to Kansas After Reconstruction, by Nell Irving Painter

Black Newspapers and the Exodusters of 1879, by Nudie E. Williams